# This Is Why You CRY

Dana Peabody

An imprint of PHOENIX International Publications, Inc.

Artwork © Shutterstock 2025 Pixoode; Dejan Dundjerski; MillaF; Davidenco; VELvector; PeopleImages.com - Yuri A; New Africa; Ascrea; AYO Production; scene_ko; tonkhao wanpiya; Anatoliy Karlyuk; svtdesign; ANURAK PONGPATIMET; Iconic Bestiary; robuart; guitarherozz; Aleksandr_Lysenko; Subject Photo; valkoinen; lenjoyeverytime; newelle; GraphicsRF; showcake; Riccardo Mayer; Sandile Simelane

Published by Sequoia Kids Media,
an imprint of Sequoia Publishing & Media, LLC

Sequoia Publishing & Media, LLC,
a division of Phoenix International Publications, Inc.

8501 West Higgins Road, Chicago, Illinois 60631
34 Seymour Street, London W1H 7JE
Heimhuder Straße 81, 20148 Hamburg



CustomerService@PhoenixInternational.com



www.PhoenixInternational.com

Library of Congress Control Number: 2024952388

ISBN: 979-8-7654-1132-2

# This Is Why You CRY

## Table of Contents



**Bold** words are explained in the glossary.

# Are your Eyes Watering?

It doesn't matter how big and brave you are; if you've ever felt sad or hurt, you've probably wanted to cry.

We all cry for lots of different reasons. It might be because we are very sad, very happy, or because our bodies are hurting.

Crying is a perfectly normal thing to do. But why do we do it?

# Types of Tears

Not all tears are the same.
We actually make three
different types of tears:

Everyone is different, and this means we cry at different things.

# Basal Tears

We always have basal tears in our eyes. They **lubricate** our eyes so that they don't get too dry. These tears are spread around the eye by blinking.

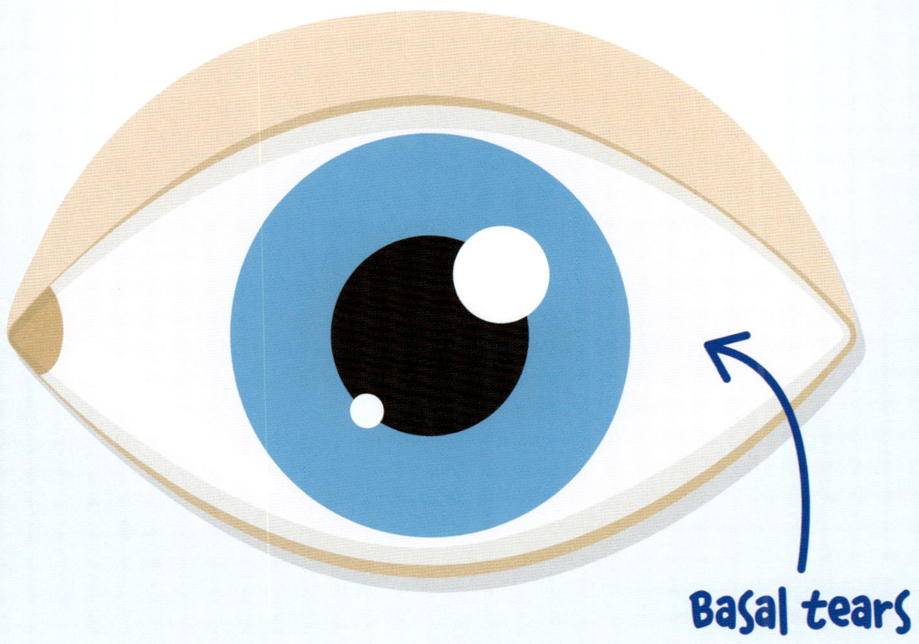

# Reflex Tears

Our bodies produce reflex tears when something **irritates** our eyes. This could be things such as **allergens** or smoke.

# Emotional Tears

We cry emotional tears when we have strong feelings or are in pain. If we hurt ourselves or feel surprised, this can make us cry emotional tears too.

We even cry emotional tears when we are very happy.

# Making Tears

The *lacrimal* (lak-ri-mul) **system** is made up of organs and body parts that allow us to make and drain away tears. The most important parts are the eyes and nose.



Organs are parts of our bodies that do certain jobs.

When we need to cry—for any reason—our brain sends a message to our body to start up our lacrimal system. We then begin to cry.

## Message sent. It's time to cry!

Let's take a look at where these tears come from and where they go.

# Journey of a Tear

**Step 1:**

The tears come out of the **LACRIMAL GLAND** behind the top of the eye.

**Step 2:**

Some tears are drained away from the eye through the **TEAR DUCT** in the corner.

**Step 3:**

These are then taken to the **LACRIMAL SAC**.

## Step 4:

The tears are then drained away through the nose. (That's why your nose gets runny when you cry!)

## Step 5:

If the duct can't drain the tears away quick enough, the tears run down your face.

When we cry, it puts a lot of stress on the muscles in our face and can give us a bad headache.

# What's in a Tear?

Tears have three layers.

## Layer one:

This oily layer stops tears from **evaporating** (ee-vap-or-ate-ing).

## Layer two:

This layer holds water and **minerals**, such as salt. (That's why your tears taste salty!)

## Layer three:

This is a layer of **mucus** that helps to keep the tear on the eye.

When we cry because of emotion or pain, other things are released by our glands. Lots of hormones build up in our bodies when we feel emotional or experience pain.

# Feeling Better?

Have you ever heard people say that they have "had a good cry"? How can crying make us feel better?

As we cry, all the stress hormones our body has built up are washed away with our tears, taking the stress out of our body.

# Eye Boogers

Sometimes we can wake up with eye boogers in the corner of our eyes. These can be dry and crusty, or wet and stringy. Both are normal!

Not all of the oil from our basal tears is washed away. Eye boogers are a mixture of this oil and any dust in our eyes.

# Gooey Eyes

Sometimes our eyes can get **infected**. They may become bloodshot, itchy, or a bit sticky from mucus. One type of eye infection is called conjunctivitis (con-junk-tiv-eye-tus).

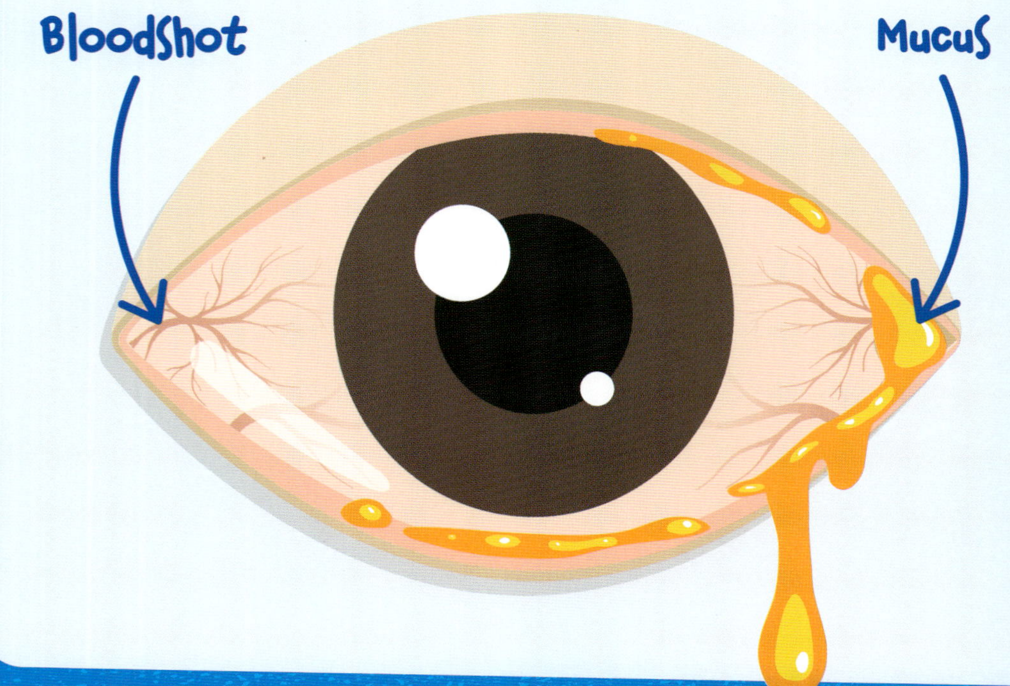

To help prevent eye infections, make sure you:
wash your hands regularly.
Don't rub your eyes too much.

# Tears Talk

Babies can't talk, so they use their tears to tell us when they need something. Most of these tears aren't because the baby is in pain, but because they need our attention.

Babies cry when they are hungry, tired, sick, or when their diapers are dirty.

# Test Your Knowledge

**Are these tears reflex or emotional?**

Answers: A. Emotional; B. Emotional; C. Emotional; D. Refle

# Glossary

**allergens:** things that cause an allergic reaction

**evaporating:** turning from a liquid into a gas or vapor, usually through heat

**infected:** when germs or disease have entered part of the body

**irritates:** when something aggravates part of the body, making it red, sore, or itchy

**lubricate:** to cover something in something slippery

**minerals:** important things that plants, animals, and humans need in order to grow

**mucus:** a slimy substance that helps to protect and lubricate certain parts of the human body

**system:** a set of things that work together to do specific jobs

# Index